What Color Is Love?

By
Colette Delacroix

What Color Is Love?   FIRST EDITION

Copyright © 2013 Colette Delacroix

To Mother and Daddy
who held me in their arms and read to me.

This book lovingly belongs to

_____ .

What color is love?

Is it brilliant blue like the sky on a cloudless day?

What color is love?

Is it gentle green
like the grass in May?

What color is love?

Is it ornate orange
like the tip of a butterfly's wing?

What color is love?

Is it playful purple
like violets blooming in spring?

What color is love?

Is it **rich red**

like an apple just out of reach?

What color is love?

Is it precious pink
like a shell brought
from the beach?

What color is love?

Is it yummy yellow
like the rays of the
sun's warm glow?

What color is love?

Is it whisper white
like a dandelion wish
ready to blow?

What color is love?

Is it **bold brown**
like the earth at the
edge of a creek?

What color is love?

Is it **boundless black**
like a mountain's peak?

What color is love?

Is it the splash of a spectrum
like a rainbow resting high?

Is love a color?

Or, is it a glorious gleam
like the light in your laughing eye?

COLETTE DELACROIX is a native and resident of New Orleans, Louisiana.
She is a multi-talented artist and writer dedicated to arts and education.
Colette holds her Master's Degree in Art Education from
Columbia University in New York City, and Bachelor's Degree in
Visual Art from Manhattanville College in Purchase, New York.

This is Colette's first children's book.

ILLUSTRATIONS
The author created each illustration in this book
individually by hand using acrylic paints on art paper.

Colette Delacroix in 1955
Age Five

Contact us:

DELABONICS BOOKS

delabonics@gmail.com

KAT TALES PUBLISHING

williamskatie370@yahoo.com